Dear Pastor

by

BILL ADLER

Thomas Nelson Publishers
Nashville

Published in Nashville, Tennessee, by Thomas Nelson, Inc., Publishers and distributed in Canada by Lawson Falle, Inc., Cambridge, Ontario.

Printed in the United States of America.

Illustrated by Bettye Beach

Library of Congress Cataloging in Publication Data

Main entry under title:

Dear Pastor.
  1. Clergy—Anecdotes, facetiae, satire, etc. 2. Children—Anecdotes, facetiae, satire, etc.
I. Adler, Bill.
PN6268.C5D4   816´.54´0809282   80-24088
ISBN 0-8407-5218-0

Dear Pastor

dear pastor,
   I like to go to church except when there is something better to do.
                    Teddy
                    Age 10
                    Needles

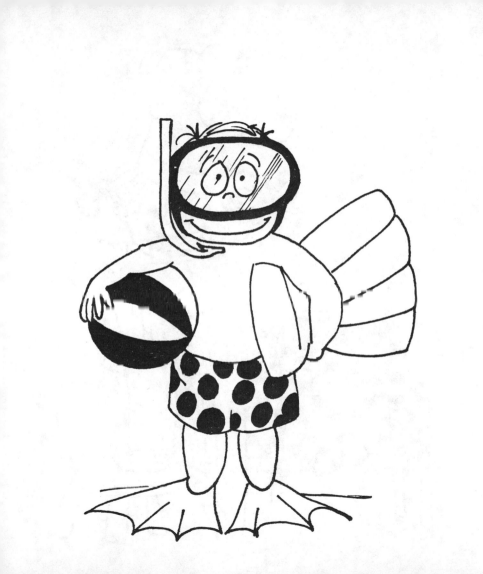

Dear Pastor,

I baked a cake for God.

Beth
Age 10
Lawrenceville

P.S. I hope He likes
chocolate cake.

Dear Pastor,

Could you SAY A Special blessing for my Aunt Beatrice. She has been looking for a husband for 12 years and still hasn't found one.

Yours sincerely,
Debbie
Age 9
Duluth

Dear Pastor,

My mother said our church is 150 years old. You sure don't look that old to me.

Sincerely yours,
Lisa
Age 9
Knoxville

Dear Pastor,
   I am a very religious person. I never do anything bad on Sunday.
          Sincerely yours,
          Roger
          Age 7
          Easthampton

Dear Pastor,

I know GOD loves everybody but He never met my Sister.

Yours sincerely
Arnold
Age 8
Nashville

Dear Pastor,
   Do I have to say grace before every meal? Even when I am only having a peanut butter and jelly sandwich?

   Wesley
   Age 9
   Baltimore

Dear Pastor

Thank YOu for your sermon
on Sunday.
I will write more   when my mother
explains to me what YOU said..

yours truly

Justin
age 9
Westport

Dear Pastor,
   I think more
people would come to
church if you moved it
to Disneyland.

Loreen
Age 9
Tacoma

Dear Pastor,
   I think more people would read the Bible if they made it a TV series.
               Beatrice
               Age 9
               York

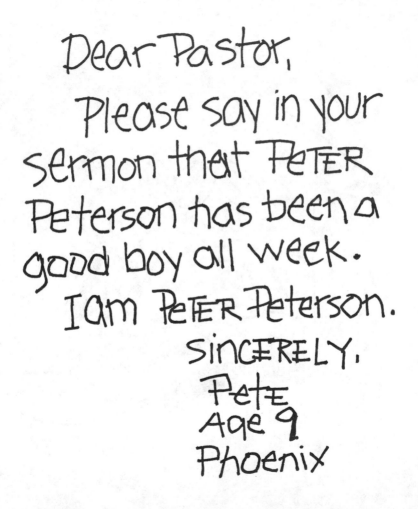

Dear Pastor,

My grandparents go to church more than anybody else in the family because they have known God longer than anybody else.

Marcia
Age 10
Buffalo

De ar pastor,

Doæ you have to pay taxes/?

Or is GOD tax exempt/?

Sincerely,

James
age 10 ——→

Seattle

Dear Pastor,

My father should be a minister. Every day he gives us a sermon about something.

Robert

Age 11

Anderson

Dear Pastor

My friend Mike says that the good Christians are the ones who sing loud in church.

Yours truly,
Bruce
Woonsocket

dear pastor,

I have been a good
Christian all my life even
when nobody was
looking and I didn't
have to.

Love,
Rosemarie
Age 10
Laramie

Dear Pastor,
    I liked your sermon where you said that good health is more important than money but I still want a raise in my allowance
                    Sincerely,
                    Eleanor
                    Age 12
                    Sarasota

DEAR PASTOR,
   PLEASE PRAY FOR
ALL THE AIRLINE PILOTS.
I AM FLYING TO CALIFOR-
NIA TOMORROW.
            LAURIE
            NEW YORK CITY
            AGE 10

Dear Pastor,
  Did God make girls smarter than boys? My big sister says so.
      yours truly,
      Ryan
      Age 9
      Grand Rapidz

Dear Pastor,

Do you think God knows my name? Even my teacher doesn't know my name, and I've been in her class for two years.

Sincerely
Franklin
Age 10
Moline

Dear pastor,

If God gives everybody brains
I think he forgot about my best friend
Mary.

Tom

age 10

Fort Wayne

Dear Pastor,

Who does GOD pray to? Is there a GOD for GOD?

Sincerely
Christopher
Age 9
Titusville

DEAR Pastor,
I hope to go to heaven someday but later than sooner.

Love,
ELLEN
Age 9
Athens

Dear Pastor,

Are there any devils on earth? I think there may be one in my class.

Carla
Age 10
Salina

DEAR PASTOR,

Please say a prayer for our Little League team. We need GOD's help or a new pitcher.

thank you,
Alexander
Age 10
Raleigh

Dear Pastor,
My father says I should learn the Ten Commandments. But I don't think I want to because we have enough rules already in my house.
Joshua
Age 10
South Pasadena

DEAR PASTOR,

I hope God gets
you a raise.

Yours truly,

Keith

Age 8

Stroudsbury

Dear Pastor,

Please ask God to stop all the wars. Like the one between Jimmy and Michael.

Sincerely,
Tricia

Shreveport
Age 8

Dear Pastor,

Please pray for me tomorrow. I think I forgot to do my homework.

Yours truly,
Stephen
Age 10
Chester

Dear Pastor,
I think God is smarter than everybody. Even Mr. Lewis my math teacher.

Margaret
Age 10
Galveston

Dear Pastor,
     I like to go to
church on Sunday
because I don't have
any choice.
          Yours truly,
          Sean
          Age 11
          Chillicothe

Dear Pastor,
When is God's birthday? I would like to send him a present.

Love,
Arlene
Age 8

Dear Pastor,

I say my prayers before I eat my supper but my mother still makes me finish my spinach and drink my milk.

Julie
Age 9
Buffalo

Dear Pastor,
My father likes to sit in the last row at church so he can sneak out during the sermon. Sometimes my mother stops him before he sneaks out — but not last Sunday.

Denise
Age 11
Jenkintown

Dear Pastor,

What does God do for fun?

Suzy
Age 7
Baldwin

Dear Pastor,
   I Like the choir in church very much except for the songs they sing.
                    Yours truly
                    Andrew
                    Age 8
                    Jackson

Dear Pastor,
   My father says GOD can do MIRACLES. IF I pass my history exam that will be a miricle.
            Sincerely yours,
            Thomas
            Age 11
            Shreveport

Dear Pastor,
    I liked your
sermon on Sunday.
Especially when it
was finished.
            Ralph
            Age 11
            Akron

Dear Pastor,
　　If God rested on the
7th day, why do kids still
have to go to Sunday
School?
　　　　　Yours sincerely
　　　　　　Jerry
　　　　　Age 8
　　　　　Duluth

Dear Pastor,

My sister and I are selling cookies to make money for the church.

So far we have sold 3 cookies.

Sincerely
Iris
Age 11
Savannah

P.S. My grandma bought 2 of them.

Dear Pastor,
   What is God's telephone number? I would like to call Him when I feel sad.

Margo
Age 10
Stillwater

DEAR   PASTOR

DOES GOD KNOW WALTER/   CRONKITE?

MY MOTHERR SAYS EVERY BODY KNOWS

WALTER/   cronKITE.

                    SINCERELY

                    JIMMY
                    AGE '8

                  milwauKEE

Dear Pastor,

How does God know the good people from the ~~the~~ bad people? Do you tell Him or does He read about it in the newspapers?

Sincerely,
Marie
Age 9
Lewiston

Dear Pastor,

I think more people would go to church on Sunday if you sold popcorn in the back like they do in the movie house.

Sincerely,

Dolly
Age 8
Waukegan

Dear Pastor,
   Does God really want me
to take a bath every day like
        my mother says?
                Stephen
                Age 11
                Massena

Dear Pastor,
I like the preachers on T.V. Maybe you should get your own t.v. program. You could be a big hit like "Mork and Mindy."
Sincerely
Harris
Age 10
Lincoln

Dear Pastor,
God is perfect.
Love,
Lane
Age 10
Honolulu

P.S. So is my mother
except when she yells.

Dear Pastor,
I'm sorry I can't leave more money in the plate at church on Sunday, but my father didn't give me a raise in my allowance.
Could you give a sermon about a raise in my allowance?
Love,
Patty
Age 10
New Haven

Dear Pastor,
 I would like you to marry me and my girlfriend when we get married someday. Anthony
   Age 10
    Youngstown

P.S. I'll let you know when I find a girlfriend.

dear Pastor,
I like the music in church a lot except I like music when it is loud.
Julia
Age 9
Framingham

P.S. Maybe you should make the music in church louder so God can hear it better.

DEAR PASTOR,
My mother is very
religious.
She goes to play Bingo at
church every week even if
she has a cold.
yours truly
Annette
Age 9
Albany

Dear Pastor,

We say grace at our house before every meal except at breakfast.

Nobody talks at breakfast.

Yours truly,
Sally
Age 11
Houston

Dear Pastor,

I would like to go to heaven someday because I know my brother won't be there.

Stephen
Age 8
Chicago

Dear Pastor,

We say grace every night before we eat dinner even when we have leftovers from the night before.

Yours truly,
Jacki
Age 9
CHICAGO

dear pastor

i would like to bring my dog to
church on sunday. she is only a mutt
but she is a good christian.

love,

victoria

age 9

new york

Dear Pastor,
   Everybody says amen after your sermon because they are glad it is over.
                    Thomas
                    Age 10
                    Smithtown

Dear Pastor,

   i know GOD Loves me but i wish He would give me an "A" on my report card so i could be sure.

Love,
Theresa
Age 8
Milwaukee

Dear Pastor,
  I think the church should advertise so more people will come to church on Sunday.
  Everybody advertises. Even the people who make things that God doesn't really like.
  Love,
  Elaine
  Agelo
  Chattanooga

Dear Pastor,
   We have three Bibles in our house. My mother reads the Bible everyday but my father reads the sports pages.
   Fred
   Age 9
   Wilmington

Dear Pastor,

I can't go to church next Sunday. Please tell God I will see Him next week.

Love,
Margaret
Age 7
New Orleans

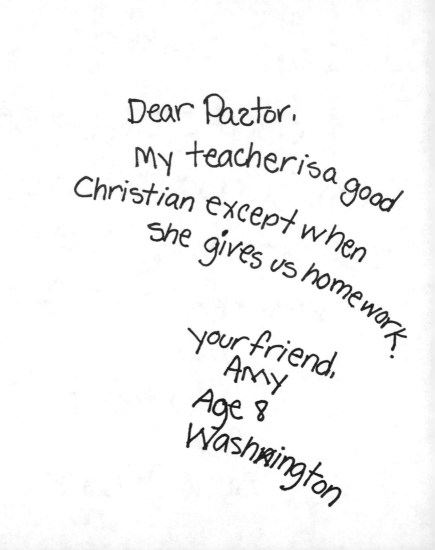

Dear Pastor,

My teacher is a good Christian except when she gives us homework.

your friend,
Amy
Age 8
Washington

Dear Pastor,

Sunday is my birthday. Please tell God.

LOVE
Teresa
Age 8
Ames, Iowa

Dere   pasttor---

iI read the bibel every day since I

was a little KId.

So far iI am up to the first page.

                    Sincrely

                    Melissa
                    age   7

                    York

Dear Pastor,
Jesus was the greatest man that ever lived. Even greater than Muhammed Ali.

Leonard
Age 6
Brooklyn

Dear Pastor,

Please say a prayer that my mother can lose 20 pounds.

She tried Weight Watchers and that didn't help. Now she needs a prayer.

Sincerely
Jennifer
Age 11
Farmington

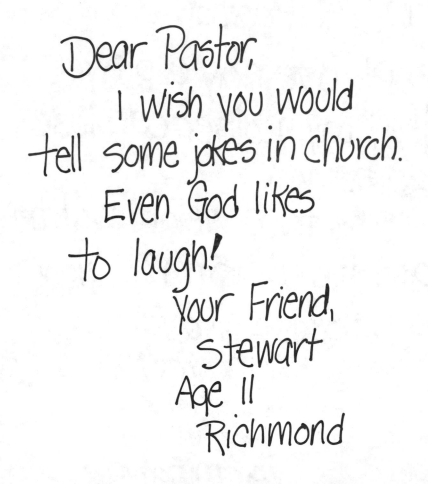

Dear Pastor,
    I wish you would
tell some jokes in church.
    Even God likes
    to laugh!
        Your Friend,
            Stewart
            Age 11
            Richmond

Dear Pastor,
   Please say a
prayer for my cat.
She is going to have
Kittens soon and I think
she is scared.
            Ellen
            Age 8
            Tuskegoj

Dere Pastor.

I wish my   father was a Pastor so he would

only have   to work one day a week too.

Yours truly.

Fred

Age   9

San Diego

Dear Pastor,

Someday I would like to sing in the choir.

My mother says I am a good singer except I can't carry a tune.

Love,
Emma
Nashville
Age 9

Dear Pastor,
 I would like to write a letter to God. Could you please tell me His zip code?
                    Edgar
                    Age 8
                    Pensacola

Dear Pastor,

Please say a prayer for my teacher. She is sick and if you said a prayer, she would get better and come back to school.

Sincerely
Susan
Age 9
Terre Haute

P.S. the other kids in my class said I shouldn't write this letter

Dear Pastor,
How much money do you collect in the plate on Sunday? I think I would like to go into that business when I grow up.

yours,
Mark
Age 7
Troy

Deer Pasxter,

I am a good Chrischun but i can't spel and add to good.

Yours truly,
Rebbeca
Age 7
Denver

Dear Pastor,

I believe God can do anything and so can my daddy.

Sincerely
Mary
Age 7
Memphis

DEAR PASTOR,

My father couldnt' give more $$$money$$$

to the chrch. HE Is a good chrischen but

he has a_CHEAP_ boss.

RONALD

AGE 10

DOYLESTOWN

Bill Adler's "letter" books have total sales of over two million copies. The collection includes such best sellers as *Letters from Camp, Kid's Letters to President Kennedy,* and more than twenty-five others. Mr. Adler lives in New York City.